THE UNOFFICIAL
HARRY POTTER
COLLEGE COOKBOOK

THE UNOFFICIAL HARRY POTTER COLLEGE COOKBOOK

A Magical Collection of Simple and
Spellbinding Recipes to Conjure in
the Common Room or the Great Hall

AURÉLIA BEAUPOMMIER

PHOTOGRAPHY BY ALINE SHAW

Skyhorse Publishing

Skyhorse Publishing books may be purchased in bulk at special discounts for sales promotion, corporate gifts, fund-raising, or educational purposes. Special editions can also be created to specifications. For details, contact the Special Sales Department, Skyhorse Publishing, 307 West 36th Street, 11th Floor, New York, NY 10018 or info@skyhorsepublishing.com.

Skyhorse® and Skyhorse Publishing® are registered trademarks of Skyhorse Publishing, Inc.®, a Delaware corporation.

Visit our website at www.skyhorsepublishing.com.

10 9 8 7 6 5 4

Library of Congress Cataloging-in-Publication Data is available on file.

Cover design by Daniel Brount
Cover photo by Aline Shaw

Print ISBN: 978-1-5107-5852-0
Ebook ISBN: 978-1-5107-5853-7

Printed in China

PUBLISHER'S DISCLAIMER:

THIS IS AN UNOFFICIAL COOKBOOK.

ALL OF THESE RECIPES WERE CREATED BY THE AUTHOR AND REFLECT HER IDEAS OF WHAT HARRY POTTER FANS MIGHT ENJOY COOKING AND EATING. THERE IS NO CONNECTION BETWEEN THE SPECIFIC RECIPES AND THE BOOKS. THEY ALL REFLECT THE AUTHOR'S IMAGINATION AND HER LOVE OF HARRY POTTER.

PROCLAMATION

Educational Decree
NO. 11-52

The Ministry reminds all first-year wizards that the use of magic is forbidden outside of school.

As such, an adult and/or N.E.W.T. level wizard is strongly encouraged to be present in order to supervise the use of certain objects to perform potentially dangerous acts and to ensure that slicing, transfers, and cooking are done without cuts, burns, or various explosions.

It is also highly advisable to use the necessary protective spells and equipment.

The Ministry would like to remind the reader (and/or legal representatives) that it is his or her responsibility to ensure both one's individual safety and that of one's guests, in particular those suffering from food allergies as well as pregnant women and witches.

The author and her representatives will not be held responsible in the event of hospitalization in the Non-Magical Wound Care or Experimental Spells Units.

On behalf of the Ministry of Magic:
A. Beaupommier

CONTENTS

INTRODUCTION

Our childhood and teenage years were spent enveloped in the magic of Hogwarts and the many extraordinary events that took place there. We trembled alongside our beloved heroes, sharing their joys, doubts, and pain, and we rejoiced in their victories, both on the Quidditch pitch and against the Dark Forces. Most important of all, because of them we learned the meaning of words like "friendship" and "loyalty."

A love of food has been a part of this story from beginning to end, like an invisible thread weaving so many different moments together, from the fabulous feasts served in the Great Hall to the sweets exchanged in the common room. But there comes a day when each of us must choose to follow our own path. So, what is to become of former Hogwarts students' stomachs when there is no longer a house-elf or attentive parent to prepare the delicious food they love so much?

Well, this book was written with you in mind. Yes, *you*, the ones who have only recently left Hogwarts and are now holding this book in your hands. Don't look so surprised! It's been prepared especially for you, whether you're studying fascinating things or beginning a thrilling new career. Yes, *you*, because you love food but have neither the space, time, nor the equipment for cooking. And most of all for *you*, because you have a tight budget.

Whether you're the person always running to catch a bus or train, an eternal latecomer, or a hardworking student, you will find something in these pages to make you happy, rain or shine!

Every one of these recipes has been concocted with love for occasions large and small, to be enjoyed alone or with friends, at home or on the go. So spread your wings, enjoy your life, and whatever you do, don't forget your snack!

Sincerely yours,

Aurélia

Unofficial Recipes Inspired By

Breakfasts

Absolutely *essential* for any good wizard hoping to start the day off right!

Burrow Muesli

EQUIPMENT

1 large bowl

1 sealed container

1 jelly jar

INGREDIENTS

serves 1 (makes 10 portions to store in a sealed container)

8 ounces (230 g) cereal (oat, corn flakes, rice, etc.)

6 tablespoons seeds (pumpkin, flax, sesame, sunflower, etc.)

1 teaspoon ground cinnamon

1 tablespoon butter, melted

5 tablespoons honey

1 vanilla bean

3 ounces (85 g) fresh fruit, canned, or defrosted

1 cup plain yogurt

Preparation Time · 10 minutes ◆ Cooking Time · 3 minutes

If your mortal enemies are prowling nearby or the ghost in the attic won't let you sleep, don't worry, this hearty muesli prepared with love will get you back to feeling your best!

◆ Concentrate and banish from your mind anything that might distract you (like the explosions and enthusiastic shouts coming from the twins' bedroom, for example . . .).

◆ Take out your bowl and add the cereal, seeds, cinnamon, melted butter, and honey. Stir together with the help of a mixing spell.

◆ Slice the vanilla bean in half lengthwise and remove the seeds by scraping the bean with the back of a knife. Add the vanilla seeds to the muesli mixture and stir again, paying no attention to the broom race taking place outside your window.

◆ Microwave for 3 minutes, stirring every minute.

◆ Let cool and store in the most tightly sealed container you have (a vault at Gringotts, Gilderoy Lockhart's autograph box, Moody's trunk . . .).

◆ To make your breakfast, rinse and peel your fruit if necessary. Add yogurt to a jelly jar, then alternate layers of fruit with layers of your homemade muesli. Enjoy immediately or close the jar and refrigerate until you have to leave.

Porridge

INGREDIENTS

serves 4

17 fluid ounces (½ l) milk

6¾ fluid ounces (20 cl) water

1 cinnamon stick

7 ounces (200 g) rolled oats

1 Granny Smith apple

Drizzle of lemon juice

2 tablespoons of honey from the Forbidden Forest

Handful of crushed hazelnuts

Preparation Time • 10 minutes ◆ *Cooking Time* • 5 minutes

◆ Heat the milk and water with the cinnamon stick in a cauldron over low heat.

◆ Sprinkle in the oats and stir clockwise for 5 minutes until the mixture is soft.

◆ Remove the cinnamon stick with a levitation charm.

◆ Rinse and peel the apple, then cut it into thin pieces. Drizzle with lemon juice, mix well, and set aside.

◆ Stir the honey into the oats with a mixing spell, pour into a bowl, top with the apples and hazelnuts, and enjoy.

Currant Cake

INGREDIENTS

serves 1

8 teaspoons oat bran

3 teaspoons vegan milk (hazelnut, oat, etc.)

1 egg

1 teaspoon baking powder

1 tablespoon maple syrup

1½ ounces (42 g) dried fruits and nuts (currants, pecans, etc.)

So, you spent too much time checking on your Polyjuice Potion project in the girls' bathroom and now you're running late. Luckily your friend the house-elf has set aside something just for you.

◆ When the house-elf knows that his friend is going to be very late, he mixes some oat bran with nondairy milk in a bowl and cracks an egg. He adds baking powder and delicious maple syrup, and whisks it together with a fork.

◆ Then, he adds his friend's favorite fruits and nuts before microwaving the mixture for 3 to 4 minutes.

◆ To be sure the cake is baked through, you must stick a knife into its center. If the cake is done, the blade will come out dry. If not, the kind elf will microwave his friend's cake for 1 more minute.

◆ The cake is turned out onto a plate and left to rest for 1 minute, then it is wrapped in a clean dish towel and given to his friend, who is running very quickly down the hallway to avoid detention.

SANDWICHES

Assorted sandwiches: for voyages on the school train, afternoons of flying broomsticks, or a thorough cleaning of the Order of the Phoenix headquarters.

Ron's Usual

INGREDIENTS
makes 4 sandwiches

8 slices whole wheat bread

9 ounces (250 g) green cabbage, thinly sliced

2 ounces (60 g) thick crème fraîche

2 ounces (60 g) traditional grain mustard

7 ounces (200 g) grated cheddar

7 ounces (200 g) corned beef

Preparation Time • 5 minutes

Unfortunately for Ron, Mrs. Weasley never remembers that her youngest son doesn't like corned beef.

◆ Using a dragon-breath spell, toast the slices of bread.

◆ Rinse the green cabbage and dry it carefully.

◆ In a small bowl, mix the crème fraîche and mustard.

◆ Spread this mixture generously on the slices of bread, then top one slice with cabbage and corned beef. Sprinkle with grated cheddar and top with a second slice of bread.

Fred and George's Merrymaking

INGREDIENTS
makes 4 sandwiches

8 slices rye bread

7 ounces (200 g) cheddar cheese (or aged gouda)

8⁴/₅ ounces (250 g) smoked trout

1 teaspoon paprika

2¹/₁₀ ounces (60 g) butter

Preparation Time • 5 minutes

◆ Cast a dragon-breath spell to toast the bread, then grate the cheddar with staccato flicks of your wand and slice the trout into strips using sharp swipes of your wand.

◆ Butter each slice of toasted bread and sprinkle with a pinch of paprika. Top with the grated cheddar and smoked trout and finish it off with the second slice of bread.

Percy's Darling

INGREDIENTS

makes 4 sandwiches

1 bunch fresh mint

3½ ounces (100 g) cooked peas

3½ ounces (100 g) fromage blanc

7 ounces (200 g) canned tuna

8 slices white bread

Preparation Time • 5 minutes

◆ Rinse and finely chop the mint leaves.

◆ Crush the peas in a bowl or use a crumbling spell. Pour in the fromage blanc and beat vigorously to give the mixture volume.

◆ Break the tuna into chunks and add the chopped mint.

◆ Spread each slice of bread with the pea purée, sprinkle generously with the tuna and mint mixture, and delicately place the second slice of bread on top, making sure the edges are perfectly aligned.

Ginny's Favorite

Preparation Time • 5 minutes ◆ *Cooking Time* • 5 minutes

INGREDIENTS
makes 4 sandwiches

8 slices white bread

7 ounces (200 g) bacon

7 ounces (200 g) sun-dried
    tomatoes

1 ball mozzarella cheese

4 tablespoons liquid honey

◆ Toast the bread until crisp and golden.

◆ In a pan, fry the bacon for 5 minutes then leave to dry with the sun-dried tomatoes on a paper towel.

◆ Slice the mozzarella into thin pieces, place a few on the first piece of toast, pour on half the honey, then add the tomatoes and bacon followed by the remaining honey and mozzarella. Top with a second slice of toast.

Charlie's Number One

INGREDIENTS

makes 4 sandwiches

8 slices country bread

7 ounces (200 g) roasted chicken

I teaspoon curry powder

3½ ounces (100 g) fromage frais

I ounce (30 g) slivered almonds

I ounce (30 g) raisins

Preparation Time • 5 minutes

◆ Cast a dragon-breath spell to toast the bread.

◆ Cut the chicken into strips using sharp swipes of your wand.

◆ In a bowl, mix together the curry powder and the fromage frais. Spread a generous helping of this mixture on each slice of bread. Then add the chicken strips, sprinkle with almonds and raisins, and top with another slice of bread.

Arthur's Delight

INGREDIENTS

makes 4 sandwiches

8 slices whole wheat bread

7 ounces (200 g) Roquefort cheese

Butter (optional)

3½ ounces (100 g) walnuts

7 ounces (200 g) grapes

Preparation Time • 5 minutes

◆ Toast the bread until crispy.

◆ Mix together the butter and Roquefort in a bowl if you prefer a softer texture.

◆ Use a crushing spell to roughly chop the walnuts.

◆ Rinse and dry the grapes and slice them in half.

◆ Spread each slice of bread with Roquefort, sprinkle with grape and walnut pieces, and top with another slice of bread.

Molly's Sweetie

Preparation Time • 10 minutes ◆ *Cooking Time* • 9 minutes

INGREDIENTS
makes 4 sandwiches

4 eggs

8 lettuce leaves

2 carrots

8 slices of bread

$2^{1}/_{10}$ ounces (60 g) mayonnaise

◆ Boil water in a small cauldron over high heat.

◆ When the first bubbles appear, carefully drop the eggs into the water and cook for 9 minutes.

◆ Rinse and dry the lettuce leaves and scrub, peel, and grate the carrots.

◆ Peel the eggs and slice with staccato flicks of your wand.

◆ Smear each slice of bread with mayonnaise then top with lettuce, eggs, and carrots before covering with a second slice of bread.

Bill's Treat

INGREDIENTS
makes 4 sandwiches

8 slices country bread

$2^{1}/_{10}$ ounces (60 g) butter

$5^{1}/_{3}$ ounces (150 g) arugula

½ bunch of radishes

8 slices roast beef (not too
    well-done)

Preparation Time • 5 minutes

◆ Cover each beautiful slice of bread with soft butter.

◆ Rinse the arugula. Wash and dry the radishes and remove the
stems. Slice in rounds.

◆ Place one slice of meat on each slice of buttered bread, sprinkle
with radish slices, and top with arugula and the final slice of bread.

Leftover Turkey Sandwiches

INGREDIENTS

serves 4

8 slices whole wheat bread

1 bunch fresh spinach leaves

3½ ounces (100 g) walnuts

18 ounces (500 g) cold cooked turkey (either from a whole roasted turkey or turkey cutlets)

1 jar of cranberry chutney

Preparation Time • 10 minutes

This filling treat is perfect after a snowball fight in the Hogwarts courtyard.

◆ With the assistance of a dragon-breath spell, toast the slices of bread.

◆ Rinse the spinach leaves, then carefully dry them and remove any stalks that are a little tough, if necessary.

◆ Use a crushing spell to crush the walnuts into large pieces.

◆ Cast a finger-shield charm and cut the turkey in thin slices or cubes, depending on your preference.

◆ Divide the ingredients equally four ways to make four sandwiches.

◆ Spread the chutney on the slices of bread (one side only).

◆ On one slice of bread sprinkle some of the walnut pieces, half of the spinach leaves, and the turkey, followed by the rest of the spinach, the rest of the walnuts, and lastly the second slice of toasted bread.

◆ Press down gently to pack everything together and serve with a large glass of pumpkin juice (p. 97).

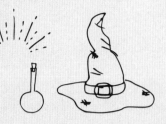

Gryffindor Sandwich

INGREDIENTS
makes 2 sandwiches

2 tomatoes

2 teaspoons mustard

4 slices white sandwich bread

2 teaspoons barbecue sauce

4 ounces (110 g) sliced cheddar cheese

Preparation Time • 5 minutes

Perfect for lunch during a Quidditch match.

◆ Rinse and slice the tomatoes with sharp flicks of your wand. Remove their cores and any parts that are very wet.

◆ Spread the mustard on two slices of bread. Do the same with the barbecue sauce on the remaining two slices of bread, but quickly because the players are coming out of the locker room.

◆ Place the tomato slices on top of the mustard-covered slices, cover with cheddar cheese, and continue tomato and cheese, finishing with cheddar on top.

◆ Place one bread slice covered with barbecue sauce on top of each sandwich and elbow your way to the front to get the best view of your team.

Slytherin Sandwich

INGREDIENTS

makes 2 sandwiches

½ cucumber

1 bunch chives, chopped

3 tablespoons cottage cheese

Salt, pepper

4 slices white sandwich bread

Preparation Time • 10 minutes

An ideal sandwich for a picnic by the lake.

◆ Peel and slice the cucumber into rounds ¼-inch thick using a Sectumsempra incantation.

◆ The real secret of this recipe is this: place the cucumber slices on a paper towel (a clean one, not one the house-elves are supposed to pick up), cover with a second paper towel, and press down gently to absorb the water.

◆ Let the cucumber slices rest between the paper towels for a few minutes while you prepare the other ingredients.

◆ Now, mix the chopped chives, cottage cheese, salt, and pepper in a bowl with your family crest on it.

◆ Spread the mixture on a slice of sandwich bread and place the cucumber slices on top, overlapping them slightly to form the snake scale armor that is the symbol of your house.

◆ Cover with a little bit more cottage cheese before placing another slice of bread on top of each sandwich.

◆ Press down gently, slice in half diagonally, and enjoy while you think about your future, which couldn't possibly be anything but brilliant.

Hufflepuff Sandwich

INGREDIENTS
makes 1 sandwich

1 egg (chicken, turkey, duck, or hippogriff, but *definitely* not dragon)

2 mushrooms

2 teaspoons whole grain mustard

2 slices white sandwich bread

Preparation Time • 10 minutes ◆ *Cooking Time* • 9 minutes

A sandwich to honor Helga, the founder of the house, who was known for her loyalty, generosity . . . and her love of food!

◆ Place the egg of your choice in a bowl and cover with lake water. Be careful: to avoid any risk of the egg exploding—which is always a nuisance—the water must reach at least 1 wand's width (1 inch) above it. Microwave on high for 9 minutes.

◆ *If you have made a mistake in choosing your egg and it is in fact a dragon egg, it will probably hatch. Don't panic! Well, at least not right away . . . Grab your fireproof cape, head toward the nearest exit, and call for help immediately.*

◆ Put on your dragon-hide gloves—or use a levitation charm—and remove the egg before plunging it immediately into a pot of cold water to stop it from cooking.

◆ While the egg is cooling, prepare the mushrooms.

◆ Examine your harvest carefully and mercilessly eliminate any toxic mushrooms (as well as any that bite fingers). Clean the rest of the mushrooms with a damp cloth. Do not run them under water; they will become saturated and turn into sponges!

◆ When they are nice and clean, remove the stems, chop the mushrooms into slices 1-inch thick, and set aside.

◆ Dry your egg and carefully peel off the shell; if you do this in a bowl of water, the liquid will keep the pieces of eggshell from sticking to your fingers.

◆ Crush the egg yolk and white in a bowl with a fork until they form large chunks.

◆ Now, add the mustard and mix again.

◆ Spread the egg salad on the slices of bread, arrange the mushroom slices with your characteristic elegance, and head off on your adventure! Or to the library, as the case may be.

UNOFFICIAL RECIPES INSPIRED BY

SOUPS

Hot or cold, sweet or spicy, these soups are a delight in any season!

Soup for the Basilisk

EQUIPMENT
1 blender

INGREDIENTS
serves 4

1 large bunch of watercress
(if out of season, use other
kinds of greens)

2 medium potatoes

34 fluid ounces (1 l) water,
separated

4 eggs

1 black olive

Preparation Time • 10 minutes   ◆   *Cooking Time* • 45 minutes

Don't be afraid to lock eyes with this soup!

◆ Kreacher rinses the watercress, breaking and removing the thick stalks.

◆ Then he washes the potatoes, peels them, and cuts them using a cut-all spell.

◆ Kreacher will gather water and heat it in a large cauldron. When large bubbles appear, he will add the potatoes to the water and let them cook for 35–40 minutes until the point of a knife can easily poke through. Then he adds the watercress and continues cooking 5 more minutes before putting everything in the blender. (Kreacher knows what he must do: Soup for the Basilisk must be as green as the Great Serpent's scales.)

◆ Kreacher boils more water in a smaller cauldron and cooks the eggs for 9 minutes exactly.

◆ Kreacher removes the eggs from the water and places them under a stream of cold water right away to crack their shells. He peels the eggs and cuts them open to remove the yolks, taking care to preserve their round shape. (Kreacher knows his masters will pay close attention to this detail.)

◆ Next, he cuts off one side of the egg yolk, so it will stay in place on the serving dish. He cuts the olive in thin slices.

◆ Kreacher places the egg yolk in the center of a shallow bowl featuring the coat of arms of his masters' family. Then he pours the soup into the bowl until it covers the bottom half of the yolk, places an olive slice on top of the yolk to resemble the Basilisk's eye, and serves it hot.

Kreacher's Parisian Onion Soup

INGREDIENTS

serves 4

2 onions

2 tablespoons butter

13½ fluid ounces (40 cl) beef stock

1 bay leaf

Pepper

4 slices sandwich bread or 1½ ounces (42 g) croutons

3 ounces (85 g) shredded cheese

Preparation Time • 5 minutes ◆ *Cooking Time* • 12 minutes

The previous servants of the very ancient and very noble family brought this recipe back from a journey with their masters to a bizarre city called Paris.

◆ Kreacher dismembers the onions and cuts, slices, and dices them into tiny, tiny, tiny, itsy, bitsy, teensy pieces.

◆ Then, he puts the butter and onions in a microwave-safe dish and microwaves them, covered, for 4 minutes on high power.

◆ After that, Kreacher adds the stock, bay leaf, and pepper, puts the lid back on the dish, and microwaves it for 6 minutes before dividing it among the beautiful soup dishes bearing his masters' family crest (without the bay leaf).

◆ He places a slice of bread on the surface of the good and very hot soup (replace with croutons if needed), sprinkles shredded cheese on top, and microwaves on high power for another 1 to 2 minutes until the cheese is melted.

Umbridge's Cold Pink Soup

EQUIPMENT
1 immersion blender

1 large bowl

INGREDIENTS
serves 2

12 ounces or 1 bunch (350 g) pink radishes

1 cup plain yogurt

1 tablespoon olive oil

Tap water if needed

Salt, pepper

Preparation Time • 5 minutes

Here is a sweet and spicy soup that is perfect for a marvelous day of inspections . . . exactly what you need!

◆ Quickly rinse the radishes, purchased exclusively from Ministry of Magic vegetable suppliers, and cut off the tops of the radishes.

◆ Chop each radish into 4 perfectly equal and identical pieces before placing in a bowl.

◆ Add the yogurt and oil, then cast a mixing spell and blend everything for 1 to 2 minutes until the mixture has a liquid consistency (if needed, add 1 tablespoon of tap water).

◆ Add salt and pepper to taste. Now you're ready to accomplish your tasks with order, rigor, and a smile!

Pumpkin Soup

EQUIPMENT

1 immersion blender

1 steam cooker or 1 standard model cauldron

INGREDIENTS

serves 4

2$\frac{1}{5}$ pounds (1 kg) various squashes (pumpkin, butternut, Hungarian blue, etc.)

1 chicken bouillon cube

Nutmeg

Salt and pepper

2$\frac{1}{10}$ ounces (60 g) thick crème fraîche

Preparation Time • 30 minutes ◆ *Cooking Time* • 45 minutes

The use of Hagrid's enchanted pumpkins is not recommended.

◆ With sharp swipes of your wand, chop the squashes into large chunks and remove the seeds.

◆ If you are using a cauldron, put on your dragon-hide gloves and carefully remove the squash skins, then place the pieces of squash in your cauldron, cover with water, crumble the bouillon cube, and cook for 45 minutes, until the squash is tender.

◆ If you are using a steam cooker, dissolve the bouillon cube in the water bowl then place the pieces of squash in the basket without removing the skin. Cook for 45 minutes, until the flesh is tender and the tip of your wand can easily poke through it. Cool for a few minutes and remove the skin by gently pulling on it, or with a severing charm.

◆ Taste and add grated nutmeg, salt, and pepper as desired.

◆ Blend the pieces of squash with a little of the cooking broth until your soup has a smooth texture. Pour into bowls, add the crème fraîche, and serve hot.

UNOFFICIAL RECIPES INSPIRED BY

MAIN COURSES

These tasty dishes come from all over the wizarding world and will help you put your heart into whatever work you may be doing.

Halloween Vegetables

INGREDIENTS

serves 6

2⅕ pounds (1 kg) potatoes

2⅕ pounds (1 kg) parsnips

2⅕ pounds (1 kg) carrots

2⅕ pounds (1 kg) onions

2⅕ pounds (1 kg) squash from the Hogwarts garden

2 tablespoons oil

1¾ ounces (50 g) butter

Salt and pepper

Preparation Time • 30 minutes ◆ *Cooking Time* • 1 hour

Dobby thinks it is a very good idea to cook these vegetables in large quantities. They are delicious, and if there are any left over (which rarely happens) they freeze quite well.

◆ Preheat your oven to 350°F (180°C, th. 6-7).

◆ Rinse and peel the potatoes, parsnips, carrots, and onions, then chop them into large cubes with sharp swipes of your wand. Carefully remove the skin of the squash and remove the seeds before cutting it into pieces in the same way.

◆ Place all of the vegetables in an ovenproof dish, drizzle with the oil, and toss to make sure all of the vegetables are coated. Sprinkle with chunks of butter and put in the oven.

◆ After 30 minutes, stir the vegetables with your wand (or a wooden spatula) and continue cooking.

◆ When the vegetables are fully cooked, they should be golden and crispy on the outside and tender on the inside.

◆ Season with salt and pepper and serve warm.

Stuffed Potatoes from the Burrow

EQUIPMENT
1 microwave-safe dish

INGREDIENTS
serves 2

2 large potatoes

8 slices bacon

7 ounces (200 g) shredded
    cheddar cheese

Pepper

Preparation Time • 5 minutes • Cooking Time • 7-10 minutes

It doesn't matter how great your worries are or how many enemies are on your trail . . . Tonight you are surrounded by friends, so enjoy the warmth of the Burrow.

◆ Use a cleaning charm to carefully wash the potatoes until you have removed any trace of dirt.

◆ With your wand or a knife, poke holes in the potatoes and microwave for 5 minutes. Your potatoes should allow themselves to be slashed open without the slightest resistance. If this is not the case, cook them for 2 to 3 minutes more.

◆ When your potatoes have finally started to listen to your demands, let them cool.

◆ Next, cut 4 slits in each potato, proceeding as follows: begin at the top and stop ½ inch from the bottom.

◆ Place a slice of bacon in each slit, folding it if needed, and sprinkle generously with cheddar cheese.

◆ Sprinkle with pepper as desired and microwave for 1 to 2 minutes until the cheese is just melted.

◆ Don't let them get cold. Bon appétit!

Great Hall Creamed Potatoes

EQUIPMENT
1 microwave-safe dish + 1 bowl

INGREDIENTS
serves 4

4 potatoes

1 teaspoon butter, melted

1 clove garlic

Salt, pepper

Pinch of nutmeg

8 fluid ounces (24 cl) whole milk or 4 fluid ounces (12 cl) skim milk + 4 fluid ounces (12 cl) heavy cream

6 ounces (170 g) shredded cheese

Preparation Time • 10 minutes ◆ Cooking Time • 12 minutes

The Hogwarts house-elves outdo themselves every day! Try this delicious recipe inspired by some of the dishes they serve at Christmas.

◆ The elves wash the potatoes from the garden with plenty of water and then brush, rinse, and dry them with care.

◆ Then, they remove the skin with a knife and cut the potatoes into thin slices but they do *not*, under any circumstances, rinse these slices because that would remove the good starch that helps thicken the sauce.

◆ The elves rub the melted butter around the dish, then peel the clove of garlic and rub it around the dish. A little, not too much.

◆ Next, the elves line the bottom of the dish with potato slices and continue layering them until there are no slices left.

◆ This is the moment when the elves add salt, pepper, and nutmeg.

◆ Then, they either add the whole milk directly to the dish or mix the skim milk and heavy cream in a separate bowl before pouring it over the potatoes.

◆ The dish then goes in the Hogwarts microwave for 10 minutes on high power.

◆ The warm-hearted elves sprinkle a little cheese on top for their student friends and cook for 2 more minutes before serving the dish immediately while it's still warm.

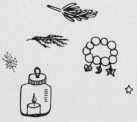

Hagrid's Baked Eggs

EQUIPMENT

1 microwave-safe dish

4 ramekins/bowls/glasses/cups
in the color of your favorite
Hogwarts house

INGREDIENTS

serves 4

8 ounces (230 g) pumpkin
(fresh or canned)

Tap water

4 slices smoked ham (or regular
ham if you can't find it)

3 ounces (85 g) mozzarella
cheese

3 ounces (85 g) crème fraîche

4 eggs

Pepper

Preparation Time • 10 minutes   ◆   *Cooking Time* • 14 minutes

Here's a recipe that the school gamekeeper likes to make when he gets home from one of his mysterious walks in the Forbidden Forest.

◆ Go out to the vegetable garden and find your shiniest and chubbiest pumpkin and roughly slice it into cubes with your wand, a knife, or a pink umbrella, depending on your mood.

◆ Remove the peel if needed and place the pumpkin pieces in a microwave-safe dish. Cover with water from the lake and microwave on high power for 8 minutes.

◆ Drain the water using a colander, fork, cheesecloth, or old sock, and set aside.

◆ Explain to your beloved dog that not all of the ham is for him and tear whatever pieces you have left into strips that are 1-inch long and ½-inch wide.

◆ Drain the mozzarella and dice it into ½-inch pieces. Add the crème fraîche and microwave for 2 minutes.

◆ Divide the pumpkin pieces into the ramekins and cover with ham strips, followed by the mozzarella-crème fraîche mixture.

◆ Crack an egg over the top, then cover and microwave each ramekin for 1 minute.

◆ Lovingly place the ramekins on a plate and serve with pepper while you enjoy a quiet conversation in front of your hut with your dearest friends.

Kreacher's Fluffy Eggs

EQUIPMENT
1 microwave-safe dish

INGREDIENTS
serves 1

2 hippogriff eggs

3 tablespoons milk

4 tablespoons shredded cheese

Salt and pepper

Preparation Time • 3 minutes ◆ *Cooking Time* • 2 minutes

Kreacher's ancestors have served this recipe to the very noble and very ancient Black family since time immemorial.

◆ Kreacher cracks the eggs by crushing their shells, then he beats and whips them in a bowl until the mixture becomes a little foamy.

◆ Only now does Kreacher add the milk, cheese, salt, and pepper, then he pours everything into the green dish bearing the crest of the very noble Black family and microwaves it for 2 minutes on high power.

◆ The omelet is to his mistress's liking once it has doubled in volume.

◆ Kreacher serves it without a moment's hesitation.

Professor Pomona Sprout's Savory Mug Cake

EQUIPMENT
1 bowl + 1 mug

INGREDIENTS
serves 1

2 tablespoons fresh spinach

1 tablespoon tap water

1½ ounces (42 g) goat cheese

1 egg

4 tablespoons milk

1 tablespoon olive oil

Pinch of baking powder

2 tablespoons cornstarch

Preparation Time • 5 minutes • Cooking Time • 5 minutes

A little something sweet with a hint of vegetal flavor—the perfect snack while you wait for the mandrakes to finish growing.

◆ Harvest some of the spinach growing in greenhouse number 2, rinse the leaves to remove any traces of dirt or tiny creatures, and place them lovingly in a bowl with 1 tablespoon of tap water. Cover and microwave for 2 minutes, then drain.

◆ With the help of a fumbleslice charm, crumble the goat cheese into small pieces, setting aside one slice for later.

◆ Mix together the egg (without its shell), milk, and oil in a mug until thoroughly combined.

◆ Next add the baking powder and flour, sifted like the finest compost, and stir again.

◆ Once you've reached this part of the recipe, reunite the pieces of goat cheese with the spinach leaves and microwave for 2 minutes.

◆ Crown your creation by placing the reserved slice of goat cheese on top and microwave for 30 more seconds.

◆ Send your students to look for an imaginary plant while you dig in.

Burrow Summer Salad

INGREDIENTS

serves 4

1 head of lettuce or 10–12 ounces (300–350 g) mixed salad greens (leaf lettuce, leftover radish leaves, dandelion greens, arugula, etc.)

4 slices bacon

1 large tomato (or 8 cherry tomatoes)

3 ounces (85 g) cheese

4 teaspoons balsamic vinegar

Pepper

2 teaspoons walnuts

Preparation Time • 10 minutes   ◆   *Cooking Time* • 30 seconds

Ah, those long summer nights spent talking with your friends about everything and nothing and listening in the distance to the owls, the grumbling gnomes, and the ghost in the attic.

Note:

In the winter, replace the summer salad greens with endives, watercress, or lamb's lettuce.

◆ Rinse the salad with water from the barrel under the drainpipe and then, to dry it easily, hop on your broom and perform a series of acrobatic tricks of your choosing.

◆ Return to solid ground, chop the largest leaves into ½-inch pieces, and set aside.

◆ Place the bacon slices on a plate, cover with an anti-projection lid, and microwave 20–30 seconds on high power until crispy.

◆ Apparate back to the drainpipe to rinse the tomato, then cut it into ½-inch cubes. Keep the juice from the tomato to make the dressing!

◆ With the help of a clipping charm, slice the cheese into ½-inch pieces.

◆ In a bowl, stir together the vinegar and reserved tomato juice. Add pepper to taste.

◆ Put some salad in each bowl and sprinkle with the diced cheese and tomatoes.

◆ Crumble the bacon and walnuts in pieces, then add them to the salad.

◆ Gently mix, add the dressing, and serve immediately.

Beauxbatons Croque-Monsieur

INGREDIENTS

serves 2

1 large slice of ham
  (around 5 ounces/140 g)

5 ounces (140 g) shredded
  cheese

4 slices sandwich bread

Pinch of nutmeg

4 ounces (110 g) butter

Preparation Time • 5 minutes ◆ *Cooking Time* • 2 minutes

This classic dish from Beauxbatons Academy of Magic is just like its students: delicate, delightful, and perfect!

◆ Slice your most beautiful piece of ham into 2 equal parts and divide the shredded cheese into 4 equal parts.

◆ Delicately place 2 slices of sandwich bread on a microwave-safe dish.

◆ Use a levitation charm to sprinkle with shredded cheese.

◆ Place the ham slices on top of the cheese and, if necessary, fold the edges so they do not extend beyond the borders of the croque-monsieur, maintaining the sandwich's reputation as the height of elegance.

◆ Sprinkle with a pinch of sweetly scented nutmeg and cover with a second portion of shredded cheese.

◆ Spread the butter with finesse over the two remaining slices of bread and use them to finish off the sandwiches, buttered side up.

◆ Microwave on high to melt the cheese.

◆ This dish is delicious with a little salad or a nice soup, depending on the season.

Umbridge's Pink Pasta

EQUIPMENT
I microwave-safe plate and bowl

INGREDIENTS
serves 4

14 ounces (400 g) pasta

Tap water

17 fluid ounces (50 cl) heavy cream

5½ ounces (156 g) tomato purée

Salt and pepper to taste

I tablespoon fresh basil leaves, finely chopped, or 2 teaspoons dried basil

Preparation Time • 3 minutes   ◆   Cooking Time • 11 minutes

Pink, pink, pink, never too much pink with this delicious pink dish!

Note:

Professor Umbridge rarely has friends over for dinner, but you never know, it could happen . . .

◆ While a student of your choosing is copying down that famous phrase "I must not tell lies . . . ," place the pasta in a dish and add water following this rule: 2 parts water to 1 part pasta.

◆ Microwave for 5 minutes on high power. Stir and microwave for 5 more minutes, drain, and set aside.

◆ Mix the heavy cream and tomato purée together in a bowl. Cover and microwave for 1 minute.

◆ Serve the pasta in your favorite bowls, the matching pink ones with kittens on them, then pour over the sauce, add salt and pepper, and sprinkle with fresh or dried basil.

Baked Leeks and Ham from the Room of Requirement

EQUIPMENT
1 microwave-safe plate

INGREDIENTS
serves 4

4 large or 6 small leeks

1 tablespoon water

4 slices of ham

4 fluid ounces (12 cl) milk

2 tablespoons crème fraîche

Pinch of nutmeg

2 ounces (55 g) shredded cheese

Preparation Time • 10 minutes   ◆   *Cooking Time* • 6 minutes

In the mood for something delicious? Try this specialty from the Room of Requirement, ideal for refueling an army of famished magicians.

◆ Use the secret passage to go and harvest a few leeks wherever you can find them.

◆ Remove the roots and separate the white parts from the green parts using a clipping charm.

◆ Next, cut the white parts of the leeks into 1-inch pieces and rinse them in lake water before placing them in a microwave-safe dish and microwaving them on high power for 3 to 4 minutes with 1 tablespoon of water. Drain the leeks and ask for the Room to appear. It will be happy to provide you with everything you need: a colander, clean sock, cheesecloth, etc.

◆ Roll the slices of ham to hold them in place (feel free to use a stupefying charm if needed) and lay them on top of the softened leeks.

◆ Beat together the milk, crème fraîche, and nutmeg in a bowl. Pour over the ham and leeks and top with shredded cheese. Cover and microwave for 2 minutes.

Unofficial Recipes Inspired By

Desserts

So deliciously spellbinding that they'll turn you into a friendly troll.

R·I·P· Cookies

EQUIPMENT
1 tombstone-shaped cookie
    cutter

INGREDIENTS
serves 4
4²/₅ ounces (125 g) flour
1 egg
2¹/₁₀ ounces (60 g) sugar
1 tablespoon vanilla extract
2¹/₁₀ ounces (60 g) butter

Preparation Time • 10 minutes + 30 minutes of resting time
Cooking Time • 10-15 minutes

No Deathday party is complete without a tombstone!

◆ Preheat your oven to 350°F (180°C, th. 6–7).

◆ With a twirl of your wand, sift the flour into a bowl, add the egg (without the shell), sugar, and vanilla extract and mix together.

◆ Cast a hot air charm to soften the butter without melting it.

◆ Stir everything together with a mixing spell until you have a smooth dough. Roll the dough into a ball, cover it in plastic wrap, and refrigerate for 30 minutes.

◆ Roll out the dough to a thickness of around 3–5 mm: use either a rolling pin or a steady sweep of your wand.

◆ Cut out the cookies with your cookie cutter and bake for around 10–15 minutes until they are a pale blond color but not yet golden brown.

◆ Remove the cookies from the oven, let cool, and serve.

Great Hall Christmas Pudding in a Bowl

Do you remember your first Christmas morning in the Great Hall? When steam smelling of raisins and cinnamon wafted through the air and the ghosts joyfully sang carols? Yes? Well then, enjoy this return to that delicious holiday atmosphere!

INGREDIENTS

serves 1

1 apple

3 tablespoons milk

1 egg

1½ ounces (42 g) flour

Pinch of baking powder

Pinch of cinnamon

1 tablespoon currants

1 tablespoon crushed almonds

1 tablespoon crushed hazelnuts

1 tablespoon walnuts

◆ Rinse the apple and cut it in half. Remove the stem, core, and seeds, then dice it into ½-inch cubes.

◆ Use a levitation charm and pour the milk into a bowl. Crack the egg into the bowl and whisk together.

◆ Add the flour, baking powder, and cinnamon, and stir.

◆ Next, incorporate the apple cubes, currants, and nuts. Mix one last time, moving your spoon around the bowl as many times as there are windows in your Advent calendar, then place your bowl in the microwave and cook on high for 3 minutes.

◆ Enjoy beside the fire or a radiator as you watch the snowflakes waltz.

Mrs. Puddifoot's Valentine's Day Dessert

EQUIPMENT
2 transparent glasses

INGREDIENTS
serves 2

1 meringue as wide as your true love's hand

3 ounces (85 g) fresh or defrosted berries (strawberries, raspberries, currants, etc.)

Whipped cream

Candy hearts for decoration (optional)

Preparation Time • 10 minutes

Ahhh, it's Valentine's Day at the legendary Mrs. Puddifoot's Tea Shop. Here's a recipe that will help you re-create its rather special romantic ambiance!

◆ Carefully break the meringue into large pieces, then rinse the berries in water as pure as your feelings and gently dry them off.

◆ Cut the largest berries into ½-inch pieces and set aside.

◆ Tenderly form a layer of meringue at the bottom of each glass, cover with the sweetest and most flavorful whipped cream possible, and top with berries. Repeat the layering and be sure to end with a layer of whipped cream.

◆ Sprinkle a few candy hearts on top (or a few pieces of fruit set aside for decoration), and enjoy as you gaze into each other's eyes.

Burrow Chocolate Cake with Vanilla Cream

INGREDIENTS
serves 8

For the cake:

7 ounces (200 g) butter

7 ounces (200 g) dark chocolate

7 ounces (200 g) sugar

7 ounces (200 g) cornstarch

2 teaspoons baking powder

6 eggs

For the vanilla cream:

14 ounces (400 g) vanilla pudding

2 tablespoons milk

Preparation Time • 5 minutes ◆ *Cooking Time* • 10 minutes

Vacation may already be over, but try this dessert and you will be instantly transported back to those beautiful summer evenings in the company of your dearest friends.

◆ Push aside the piles of books and school supplies on the table and place the butter and chocolate pieces in a large bowl. Cover and microwave for 2 to 3 minutes until melted.

◆ Respond to the plaintive cries from upstairs that the wizard robes aren't dry yet but that they will be ready for tomorrow.

◆ Take your bowl out of the microwave without burning yourself and stir in the sugar, cornstarch, and baking powder. Crack the eggs and incorporate them without their shells.

◆ Microwave 5 to 7 minutes on high power.

◆ Duck to avoid the rolls of parchment flying in your direction and stick your wand into the center of the cake; it should come out creamy (if this is not the case, continue cooking for 1 to 2 minutes).

◆ Pour the vanilla pudding into a bowl, add a little milk if it is too thick, and warm for 1 to 2 minutes in the microwave.

◆ Serve with slices of cake and try not to think about the objects that have mysteriously disappeared and the suitcases that are stubbornly refusing to close.

Great Hall Stuffed Apples

INGREDIENTS

serves 1

1 apple

1 tablespoon vanilla ice cream

1 tablespoon caramel sauce

1 tablespoon crushed hazelnuts

Preparation Time • 5 minutes   ◆   Cooking Time • 2 minutes

Sweet Hogwarts autumn, the season for comforting desserts.

◆ Consult the Marauder's Map to make sure there is no one around and slip out behind a coat of armor to go pick up an apple in Hogsmeade.

◆ Rinse the apple and then, with the help of a perforation charm, remove core and seeds by digging a cylinder-shaped hole in the center; your apple should remain whole with a hole in the center opening at both ends like the castle's secret passages.

◆ Place the apple on a plate, cover, and microwave for 2 minutes while you explain to the person in the portrait on the wall that your comings and goings must remain a secret.

◆ Spoon the vanilla ice cream into the center of the apple, cover with caramel sauce, and sprinkle with crushed hazelnuts.

◆ Serve immediately without worrying about any of your upcoming exams.

Room of Requirement Pear and Chocolate Mug Cake

EQUIPMENT
2 mugs

INGREDIENTS
serves 1 courageous member of the Order

1 pear

2 tablespoons water, divided

2 tablespoons granulated sugar, divided

¾ ounce (21 g) chocolate pieces

2 tablespoons cornstarch

Pinch of baking powder

1 egg

1 tablespoon milk

1 teaspoon butter

Preparation Time • 5 minutes ◆ Cooking Time • 5 minutes

Need some encouragement after a hard day? Whether you've been working tirelessly to master the most arduous spells, each one more difficult than the next, or if you have recently escaped even greater dangers, it's time to treat yourself.

◆ Since you're in the Room of Requirement, take advantage of the space and equipment available to you for cooking!

◆ Rinse the pear, peel it, and then, with the sharpest knife you can find—or your wand and a chopping charm—slice it into small ½-inch pieces.

◆ Add the pear pieces to a mug along with a tablespoon each of water and sugar.

◆ Microwave for 3 minutes.

◆ In another mug, melt the chocolate with the remaining tablespoon of water for around 30 seconds.

◆ Next add the remaining sugar, cornstarch, baking powder, egg, milk, butter, duck your head to avoid any spells with unfortunate trajectories, and whisk vigorously with a stirring charm until the mixture has a uniform texture.

◆ Add the pears and mix again.

◆ Cook the mixture for 2 minutes in the microwave and enjoy with friends, hidden safely in the secret room.

Umbridge's Pink Mug Cake

EQUIPMENT
1 mug

INGREDIENTS
serves 1

2 pinches of baking powder

1 teaspoon butter

½ teaspoon vanilla extract

2 tablespoons vanilla sugar

4 fluid ounces (12 cl) of your favorite red/pink fruit juice (strawberry, raspberry, etc.)

1 egg

Preparation Time • 2 minutes + 3 minutes rest ◆ *Cooking Time* • 2 minutes

Quieting unseemly rumors and making sure that dear Cornelius's directives are all being carried out in proper fashion is selfless work. Take a moment for yourself by enjoying this delicious cake and you will be all the more ready to continue your work . . .

◆ Find your favorite mug—the pink one with kittens on it that Cornelius gave you, for example—and combine all of the ingredients in it. Make sure your every action is ruled by order and discipline! Start with the baking powder and continue with the butter, vanilla extract, vanilla sugar, fruit juice, and the egg. You are aware, of course, that it would be perfectly ludicrous to keep the eggshells. Get rid of them.

◆ Beat the mixture mercilessly until every ingredient has lost its individuality.

◆ Microwave for 30 seconds. Let rest for 30 seconds. Continue this process until the cake has cooked for 2 minutes.

◆ Let rest for 1 minute and 30 seconds and plunge your knife into the center with delight.

◆ This recipe is for 1 person; it's too good to share!

Canary Creams

EQUIPMENT
4 ramekins

INGREDIENTS
serves 4

2 gelatin sheets

2 tablespoons lemon juice

8⁴/₅ ounces (250 g) liquid crème fraîche

1¾ ounces (50 g) sugar

2¹/₁₀ ounces (60 g) ground almonds

1 ounce (30 g) lemon peel, not treated with growth serum or No-Pest Spray

Preparation Time • 20 minutes + 1 hour of resting time
Cooking Time • 5 minutes

Unlike Fred and George's successful joke, these delicious treats will not make you sprout feathers.

◆ Soften the gelatin sheets in a bowl of water for 15 minutes.

◆ Place a small cauldron over low heat.

◆ Pour in the lemon juice, crème fraîche, and sugar. Mix well.

◆ Next add the ground almonds and the lemon peel and stir again with a mixing spell while imitating the song of the canary (this step is absolutely essential to the success of this recipe).

◆ Wring out the gelatin sheets by pressing them gently between your hands and add them to the cauldron.

◆ Fill the ramekins, recite a plumage spell with the seriousness required, and chill for 1 hour.

Hogwarts-Style Snowballs

EQUIPMENT
1 whisk
Plastic wrap

INGREDIENTS
serves 4

O.W.L. Level Wizards:
4 egg whites
Pinch of salt
1 jar vanilla custard
2 tablespoons milk
Powdered sugar for decoration

N.E.W.T. Level Wizards:
4 egg whites
Pinch of salt
1 vanilla bean
8½ fluid ounces (¼ l) whole milk
2 egg yolks
1¾ ounces (50 g) granulated sugar
Powdered sugar for decoration

Preparation and Cooking Time • 5 minutes + 20 minutes

For all wizards:
◆ Crack the eggs and pour the whites into a bowl with a pinch of salt. Cast a frothing spell or use an electric beater to beat the whites into stiff peaks. The whites are ready when you can turn the bowl over above your head without finding yourself wearing a white and moussey hat.

◆ Next, place a sheet of plastic wrap in a separate bowl, leaving plenty of extra hanging over the edge. Pour in one quarter of the beaten egg whites and close the plastic wrap over them to form a small ball. Microwave for 30–45 seconds until firm.

◆ Repeat the same process to make 4 snowballs. Let cool.

◆ Cut the snowballs in half, and using a small spoon or a gouging spell scoop out the center of four of the half-spheres, leaving a border three-quarters of an inch (2 cm) thick to prevent any unwanted holes.

Preparation of the custard for O.W.L. level wizards:
◆ Dilute the vanilla custard with the milk.

Preparation of the custard for N.E.W.T. level wizards:
◆ Cut the vanilla bean in half lengthwise. With the back of a knife, scrape the two halves to remove the seeds.

◆ Place a standard model cauldron over high heat with an upturned saucer on the bottom (this will keep the milk from sticking to the bottom of the cauldron). Pour in the milk and bring to a boil, watching carefully. You can use one of your professor's favorite mottos: "Constant vigilance!"

◆ Pour the egg yolks and sugar into a bowl, whisk until the mixture turns white, and add a small amount of the boiling milk a little at a time. (This is to heat up the eggs without scrambling them.)

(continued)

◆ Lower the heat and pour this mixture back into your cauldron of boiling milk, adding the vanilla seeds and bean. Stir with a wooden spoon and cook at very low heat for 5 minutes.

◆ To check if the custard is ready, stir then immediately run your finger through the leftovers on the back of the spoon. The custard is thick enough if the line you traced is still visible. If this is not the case, cook for a little bit longer.

For all wizards:
◆ Place the hollow half of each snowball on a plate, fill with vanilla custard, and cover with the other half-sphere.

◆ Sprinkle with powdered sugar and enjoy immediately.

Quidditch Treats

The secret weapon of the greatest athletes!

Note:

If you have any crumbs left over, or if some of the treats have broken, add the pieces to plain yogurt for your morning muesli. Absolutely delicious!

EQUIPMENT
1 silicone mold

INGREDIENTS
makes 6 treats

1 tablespoon butter

1 tablespoon granulated sugar

3 tablespoons oatmeal

1 tablespoon ground almonds

2 ounces (55 g) chocolate

1 teaspoon oil

◆ Place the butter in a bowl with your team's colors on it and melt it (the butter, not the bowl) for 15 seconds in the microwave.

◆ Next add the sugar, oatmeal, and ground almonds and stir well using a spoon or blending charm (if using the blending charm, be careful not to get the mixture all over the place—don't forget you're the one who will be cleaning up afterward!).

◆ Pour the mixture into a silicone mold in the shape of your choosing and microwave for 3 minutes on high power.

◆ Let cool 15 minutes on the corner of your desk or, in snowy or windy weather, 5 minutes on the windowsill.

◆ After cleaning out the first bowl, use it to melt the chocolate in the microwave in the following manner: 30 seconds cooking, 30 seconds rest, 30 seconds cooking, and another 30 seconds rest.

◆ Once the chocolate is completely melted, add the oil and stir gently until the mixture has a uniform and smooth texture like the feathers of a baby hippogriff.

◆ Pour the chocolate over the oatmeal mixture and set aside for 30 minutes at room temperature or 10 minutes on your windowsill.

◆ Once the chocolate has hardened, transfer it carefully onto a plate.

◆ Take concentrated aim with your wand and cut out 6 bars as equal in size as possible.

◆ Hop on your broom and watch out for Bludgers!

Cornelius's Fudge

EQUIPMENT
1 (8-inch) square dish
Parchment paper
1 sealed container

INGREDIENTS
makes 30 pieces
2½ ounces (70 g) crushed walnuts
20 ounces (570 g) chocolate pieces
14 ounces (400 g) sweetened condensed milk
10 ounces (280 g) castor sugar
1 teaspoon vanilla extract

The minister of magic's guilty pleasure!

◆ In between your two meetings and the three memos you have to write, hurry up and line the bottom and sides of your dish with parchment paper!

◆ Use a levitation charm and mix all of the ingredients together in a bowl.

◆ Microwave for 3 minutes and mix again.

◆ Pour the mixture into the 8-inch square dish (the one you keep in your secret desk drawer for precisely this purpose), smooth out the top with a flattening charm, and let cool for 2 hours.

◆ Trace 6 horizontal lines and 6 vertical lines and cut out your fudge squares (or, if you have them, use the cookie cutter of your choice).

◆ Store in a sealed container and enjoy whenever the need arises!

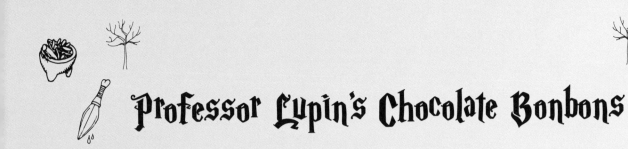

Professor Lupin's Chocolate Bonbons

INGREDIENTS

serves 6

7 ounces (200 g) baking chocolate

3½ ounces (100 g) butter

3½ ounces (100 g) powdered sugar

1 egg

1¾ ounces (50 g) ground hazelnuts

Preparation Time · 10 minutes + 15 minutes of resting time

Indispensable in the event of a Dementor attack!

◆ Place a large cauldron full of water over low heat.

◆ With the help of a crushing spell, break the chocolate into large pieces, then cut the butter into cubes. Pour the chocolate and butter into a small cauldron that you will place on top of the larger one so the heat of the water can gently melt the butter and chocolate together. Stir regularly with your wand (or a spoon).

◆ When the mixture is completely melted and warm, pour it into a dish and add the sugar and the egg. Combine and allow to cool for 15 minutes in a very cold place to allow the mixture to harden.

◆ Prepare two plates: one for the ground hazelnuts and the other to hold the bonbons.

◆ Use a small spoon to form walnut-size balls of the mixture. Roll the balls in the ground hazelnuts and place them on the second plate.

◆ These bonbons can be kept for 3 days in the refrigerator (a sort of ice chest used by non-magical people that runs on electricity).

Pink Coconut Ices

Equipment
1 large dish
Parchment paper

Ingredients
makes 15 treats

8⅘ ounces (250 g) powdered
  sugar

7 ounces (200 g) unsweetened
  condensed milk

1 pound (450 g) shredded
  coconut

Rainbow sprinkles for
  decoration

Preparation Time • 5 minutes + 2 hours resting time

◆ Use a mixing spell to stir the powdered sugar, condensed milk, and shredded coconut together until the mixture has a uniform consistency.

◆ Line the dish with parchment paper and cover with the coconut mixture, carefully smoothing it out before chilling for at least 2 hours.

◆ Now cut into cubes and roll in rainbow sprinkles.

◆ Keep refrigerated or cast a freezing charm.

Chocoballs

INGREDIENTS

serves 6

7 ounces (200 g) baking
  chocolate

3½ ounces (100 g) butter

3½ ounces (100 g) powdered
  sugar

3½ ounces (100 g)
  unsweetened puffed rice

Chocolate sprinkles for
  decoration

Preparation Time • 20 minutes + 30 minutes of resting time

◆ Break the chocolate into large pieces with the help of a crushing spell.

◆ Fill a large model cauldron with clear water, then place a small cauldron on top of it, making sure that the water level remains high enough to touch the base of the small cauldron. Add the chocolate pieces and butter to the small cauldron and gently melt over low heat. When the mixture forms a smooth ribbon, pour it into a bowl and add the sugar and puffed rice.

◆ Combine with a mixing spell and chill for 30 minutes until the mixture is firm.

◆ Scoop out a spoonful of the mixture and roll it between your hands to form a small ball.

◆ Roll the chocoballs in chocolate sprinkles and keep refrigerated.

Butterbeer Ice Cream

EQUIPMENT
1 piping bag
Parchment paper

INGREDIENTS
serves 4

3½ ounces (100 g) vanilla ice cream

3½ ounces (100 g) whipped cream

2 fluid ounces (60 ml) butterscotch syrup

2¹/₁₀ ounces (60 g) chopped hazelnuts

Preparation and Cooking Time • 5 minutes

A success since 1588!

◆ Transfer the ice cream to your piping bag and gently pipe pretty spirals into your serving cups.

◆ With an unwavering whirl of your wand, cover the ice cream with whipped cream, then, with a gentle flick of your wand, drizzle the syrup over it.

◆ Sprinkle with hazelnuts and serve very soon.

Bezoars

Preparation Time • 20 minutes + 1 hour and 30 minutes of resting time
Cooking Time • 20 minutes

Effect:

Acts as an antidote to most potions.

EQUIPMENT

1 rectangular mold around 11 x 7 inches (28 x 18 cm)

Parchment paper

1 dampened paintbrush

Dragon-hide gloves

INGREDIENTS
makes 15 stones

INGREDIENTS FOR WIZARDS

Mermaid scale powder

Dragon marrow

Full moon ray

Fairy fountain water

Powdered bicorn horn

INGREDIENTS FOR NON-MAGICAL PEOPLE

6⅓ ounces (180 g) sugar

3 tablespoons molasses

2 teaspoons honey

2 fluid ounces (60 ml) water

1 teaspoon baking soda

♦ Mix together the mermaid scale powder (sugar), the dragon marrow (molasses), the moon ray (honey), and the water in a wide large model cauldron set over a low flame.

♦ Stir *without bring to a boil* until the mermaid scale powder (sugar) is completely dissolved.

♦ Dampen your paintbrush with a gentle hydration charm and draw it along the sides of your cauldron to remove any crystals that may have formed, then bring the mixture to a boil. When bubbles appear, let simmer for 7 minutes, not stirring, until the mixture takes on a pale caramel color.

♦ Put on your dragon-hide gloves and remove the cauldron from the fire.

♦ Pour in the powdered bicorn horn (baking soda) and stir until the mixture begins to froth and doubles in volume.

♦ Line your mold with parchment paper, carefully pour in your caramel mixture, and let rest for 1 hour 30 minutes until it has hardened.

♦ Remove from the mold and cut in pieces.

UNOFFICIAL RECIPES INSPIRED BY

DRINKS

Whether you're drinking a toast to the Dark Lord or celebrating the victory of the Order of Merlin, let's raise a glass to Magic! Cheers!

Delicious Eyes

EQUIPMENT
A transparent glass for
each guest

INGREDIENTS
serves 6

1 can whole pitted lychees

1 bunch red grapes (if out of
season, use prunes instead)

34 fluid ounces (1 l) raspberry
juice

Preparation Time • **10** minutes

- ◆ Drain the lychees with a drying spell (or a colander) and set aside the juice (it might be useful to you later).

- ◆ Rinse the grapes, then stuff one in each lychee to form the pupil of the eye.

- ◆ Place the eyes in the glasses and fill with raspberry juice.

- ◆ Serve chilled.

Pumpkin Juice

INGREDIENTS
makes 1 pitcher

34 fluid ounces (1 l) apple juice

8⁴/₅ ounces (250 g) fresh pumpkin flesh (frozen if out of season)

4²/₅ ounces (125 g) apricot jam

1 wand tip of cinnamon (= 1 pinch)

Preparation Time • 5 minutes

Served at every meal!

◆ Pour all of the ingredients except the cinnamon into a standard model cauldron of medium size and combine with swirl of your wand (or an immersion blender) until the mixture has a uniform consistency.

◆ Add the pinch of cinnamon and serve chilled.

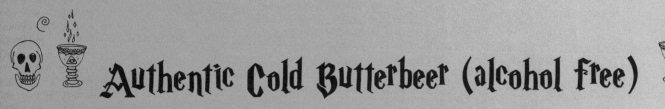

Authentic Cold Butterbeer (alcohol free)

INGREDIENTS
serves 4

17 fluid ounces (500 ml) milk

2 fluid ounces (60 ml) butterscotch syrup

cream soda

Whipped cream, if desired

Preparation Time • 5 minutes

The best thing after an evening of hard work at 12 Grimmauld Place.

◆ With a languid sweep of your wand, pour the butterscotch syrup into mugs followed by chilled cream soda.

◆ Stir gently, top with a generous helping of whipped cream, and enjoy.

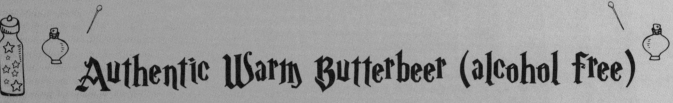

Authentic Warm Butterbeer (alcohol free)

INGREDIENTS
serves 4

17 fluid ounces (½ l) milk

2 fluid ounces (60 ml) butterscotch syrup

Whipped cream (not overly beaten), if desired

Preparation Time • 5 minutes • *Cooking Time* • 5 minutes

Drink this creamy beverage to ward off the chill of the dreariest winter day.

◆ Warm the milk in a standard model cauldron.

◆ Pour the milk into mugs, then add the syrup and stir gently with your wand (or a spoon).

◆ Add the whipped cream if desired and serve immediately.

Liquid Luck

INGREDIENTS
makes 1 vial of 17 fluid ounces (500 ml)

INGREDIENTS FOR
WIZARDS
Ubull juice

Full moon ray

Rutacé juice

Salamaga peel

Branch of musky faribola

INGREDIENTS FOR
NON-MAGICAL PEOPLE
13½ fluid ounces (40 cl) apple juice

1 small sprig of thyme

1 cinnamon stick

Juice of 1 lemon

1 tablespoon white honey

Preparation Time • 10 minutes

Effect:

Renders every action undertaken for the duration of the potion successful.

Side Effects:

Excessive self-confidence.

◆ Gently heat the ubull juice (apple) over low heat in a standard model cauldron.

◆ Strip the branch of musky faribola (thyme) and sprinkle in the leaves with your left hand.

◆ Next add the salamaga peel (cinnamon), the rutacé juice (lemon), and the full moon ray (honey).

◆ Stir, making a "figure-eight" shape with your wand, until the full moon ray (honey) is completely melted.

◆ Simmer for 5 minutes and strain.

◆ Your potion should be a luminous golden color.

Truth Serum

INGREDIENTS
makes 1 vial of 17 fluid ounces (500 ml)

INGREDIENTS FOR WIZARDS

Water from Loch Ness

Rutacé juice

Mara elegancia berries

Sinople leaves

INGREDIENTS FOR NON-MAGICAL PEOPLE

1⅓ fluid ounces (40 ml) spring water

Juice of 1 lemon

3 strawberries

1 bunch of fresh mint

Preparation Time • 21 minutes + 30 minutes of resting time

Effect:

Forces the person who ingests the elixir to reveal all of his or her secrets.

Side Effects:

Excessive honesty until the potion has completely worn off.

◆ Select only the purest sinople leaves when harvesting near a unicorn's favorite sleeping place.

◆ After filtering the water from Loch Ness, heat it for 5 minutes 55 seconds.

◆ While the water heats, extract the rutacé juice (lemon) and cut the mara elegancia berries (strawberries) in quarters.

◆ Plunge the mara elegancia pieces (strawberries) and the rubbed sinople leaves (mint) into the cauldron, stir three times clockwise, and add the rutacé juice.

◆ Brew for 15 minutes then chill for 30 minutes and strain.

◆ The potion should be colorless, odorless, and have a totally irresistible flavor.

Love Potion

INGREDIENTS
makes 1 vial of 17 fluid ounces
(500 ml)

INGREDIENTS FOR
WIZARDS
Venus kiss extract

Cupid laughter bulbs

Sysimbre juice

INGREDIENTS FOR
NON-MAGICAL PEOPLE
6¾ fluid ounces (20 cl) lychee
juice

3²/₅ fluid ounces (10 cl)
raspberry syrup

10¹/₁₀ fluid ounces (30 cl)
lemon soda

Effect:

Gives the illusion of true love to whoever drinks it without ever, alas, actually producing it.

Side Effects:

Obsessive infatuation.

Note:

The scent of the potion is different for each person, depending on what attracts him or her the most.

◆ On the day of the week dedicated to Venus, and ideally on February 14th, extract the juice from the Cupid laughter bulbs (lychees).

◆ Hold your magic wand pointing toward your heart and prepare the potion as you recite a love poem, an ode of your own creation, or a romantic song.

◆ Pour the Venus kiss extract (raspberry) into a small cauldron, gently stir in the Cupid laughter juice, and lastly add the sysimbre juice (lemon soda).

◆ Your potion will turn a pearly color and will fill with tiny bubbles rising in a graceful spiral.

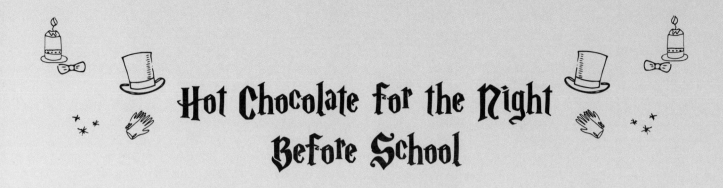

Hot Chocolate for the Night Before School

INGREDIENTS
serves 6

17 fluid ounces (½ l) milk

3⅕ ounces (90 g) honey

3⅕ ounces (90 g) cocoa

18 ounces (500 g) whipped cream

Preparation Time • 10 minutes

◆ Pour the milk into a small cauldron. Add the honey and warm slightly.

◆ Add the cocoa with a twirl of your wand and gently stir, holding your wand in your left hand.

◆ Top with whipped cream and serve immediately.

Stan's Specialty

INGREDIENTS

serves 4

34 fluid ounces (1 l) milk

5⅓ ounces (150 g) dark chocolate

1 vanilla bean

4 tablespoons sugar

1 cinnamon stick

1 teaspoon ground ginger

Preparation and Cooking Time • 20 minutes

Keep a good hold of your mug—
The Knight Bus guarantees a bumpy ride!

◆ Pour the milk into a cauldron suitable for traveling on the Knight Bus.

◆ Heat over a very low flame to keep any milk from evaporating (and to keep its whistling sound from terrifying other passengers).

◆ Using a crushing spell, break the chocolate into pieces and add to the milk.

◆ Allow the chocolate to melt gently in order to avoid splatters on the floor of the bus.

◆ Slice the vanilla bean lengthwise. (The gouging spell is a bad idea—if the bus suddenly goes over a bump this could make holes in the curtains).

◆ Scrape the bean to collect the seeds, then add the bean and seeds to the cauldron.

◆ When the chocolate is melted, add the sugar, cinnamon, and ginger. Simmer for 10 minutes, stirring gently. Remove the vanilla beans and the cinnamon stick and pour into mugs. (Do not use the levitation charm when the bus slows down. The driver still hasn't gotten over the last time . . .)

Elf Wine (alcohol free)

INGREDIENTS

serves 4

1 orange

17 fluid ounces (50 cl) grape juice

$10^{1}/_{10}$ fluid ounces (30 cl) water

4 tablespoons brown sugar

Handful of blueberries (frozen if out of season)

1 teaspoon ground ginger

1 teaspoon ground nutmeg

1 cinnamon stick

1 star anise, whole

Preparation Time • 5 minutes + 1 hour of resting time
Cooking Time • 5 minutes

Perfect for toasting to the Dark Lord.

◆ With a sharp knife, Kreacher skins the orange and cuts the flesh into quarters.

◆ Beginning with a blood-red grape juice, he pours all of the ingredients into a cauldron, boils the mixture for 5 minutes, then removes the cauldron from the fire and allows it to rest for 1 hour, stirring occasionally.

◆ After this, Kreacher filters the mixture and serves it hot or cold, depending on the desires of his masters.

Dementor's Kiss (alcohol free)

INGREDIENTS

serves 6

$10^{1/10}$ fluid ounces (30 cl) ice-cold mint syrup

34 fluid ounces (1 l) lemon juice

Preparation Time • 2 minutes

A chilling drink, much like the effect of the dementors.

◆ Kreacher pours the syrup into the beautiful glasses of his masters and dilutes it ever so slightly with the lemon juice to keep the color as murky and greenish as possible.

◆ The masters like it when Kreacher serves them this drink on ice.

Beautification Potion

INGREDIENTS
makes 1 vial of 17 fluid ounces (500 ml)

INGREDIENTS FOR WIZARDS
Pastinaca roots

Ubull juice

Salagama peel

Snow White powder

INGREDIENTS FOR NON-MAGICAL PEOPLE
13½ fluid ounces (40 cl) carrot juice

3²/₅ fluid ounces (10 cl) apple juice

1 tablespoon ground hazelnuts

1 cinnamon stick

Preparation Time • 15 minutes • Cooking Time • 15 minutes

Effect:

Reveals on the exterior the internal beauty of whoever drinks the potion.

Side Effects:

Tendency to stare at oneself in any object with a reflective surface.

◆ Rinse and peel the pastinaca roots (carrots), cook them for 10 minutes in very hot water to extract their juice, then strain.

◆ In a small cauldron over a low flame, mix the pastinaca juice (carrot juice) with the ubull juice (apple juice).

◆ Gently stir with your left hand the same number of times as the day of your birth (three times if you were born on the third, etc.).

◆ When the mixture is warm, sprinkle the Snow White powder (ground hazelnuts) into the cauldron, add the salagama peel (cinnamon) and brew for 15 minutes before removing the peel.

◆ This potion can be consumed hot or cold.